WHAT EVERY TEACHER NEEDS TO KNOW ABOUT

Classroom Environment

Developed by the
Christian Education Staff
of The General Board of Discipleship
of The United Methodist Church

DISCIPLESHIP RESOURCES

P.O. BOX 340003 • NASHVILLE, TN 37203-0003
www.discipleshipresources.org

This booklet was developed by the Christian Education Staff of The General Board of Discipleship of The United Methodist Church. It is one in a series of booklets designed to provide essential knowledge for teachers. Members of the staff who helped write and develop this series are Terry Carty, Bill Crenshaw, Donna Gaither, Rick Gentzler, Mary Alice Gran, Susan Hay, Betsey Heavner, Diana Hynson, Carol Krau, MaryJane Pierce Norton, Deb Smith, Julia Wallace, and Linda Whited.

Cover and book design by Joey McNair
Cover illustration by Mike Drake

Edited by Debra D. Smith and Cindy S. Harris

ISBN 0-88177-370-0

DR370

Contents

This booklet is dedicated to
YOU,
a teacher of
children, youth, or adults,
WHO,
with fear, excitement, joy,
and commitment,
allows God *to lead you*
in the call to
TEACH.

The gifts he gave were that some would be . . .
teachers, . . . for building up the body of Christ.
(Ephesians 4:11-12)

Introduction

Walk down a quiet hall, unlock a classroom door, and enter the room. Instantly you know that something exciting is happening here, or that the class members who use this room care about others, or that this is a class for three-year-olds (or adults, or youth)—or that no one cares about what happens in this room! Walk into any classroom and feel welcomed by it—or grateful to leave it. Any classroom speaks, even when empty of people. But when a classroom is filled with people, it speaks volumes. It becomes more than the room itself. What does your classroom say? This booklet is a guide for helping you, the teacher, set the physical and spiritual environment for Christian learning.

Teachers and small-group leaders are growing in faith. As teachers, we pay attention to our relationships with God and with others. We seek to live our faith in our daily lives. We create safe, healthy settings for people to seek God, to respond to God's grace, and to find support and encouragement for living as disciples in the world.

Growing in faith, which helps us become spiritual leaders, is a life-changing experience that continues throughout life. We grow in faith not alone but with the help of God, and with the help of our congregations, who support us by providing opportunities for learning, resources for teaching, prayer, and training.

This booklet is one of ten that will equip you for teaching. Use the entire series to reinforce your own knowledge, skills, and abilities.

Other booklets in this series are
What Every Teacher Needs to Know About

- *the Bible*
- *Christian Heritage*
- *Curriculum*
- *Faith Language*
- *Living the Faith*
- *People*
- *Teaching*
- *Theology*
- *The United Methodist Church*

Keys to a Hospitable Environment

I was glad when they said to me,
"Let us go to the house of the Lord!"

(Psalm 122:1)

We want our rooms to be places that our students—of any age—will want to return to. We want our students to feel that, *This is my place to belong, to learn, to find God.*

A Friendly Voice Calls

Whoever enters the room first has control of the classroom, so be the first person to arrive. Being first in the room allows you to make certain that the room is ready for the students, to welcome the students, and to have learning opportunities or organized fellowship prepared in order to set the tone for the time to follow. For teenagers and adults, having doughnuts, juice or coffee, and a friendly presence available may be sufficient. If you are chronically late, recruit someone to arrive early to provide the needed presence.

Greet or acknowledge every person who enters the room. It is a lonely feeling to walk into a room and find that no one notices. It is easy for those who have already arrived to become complacent when deep in conversation with others, but it is important that every person be personally greeted or acknowledged in some positive way. Some classes have designated greeters who are assigned the task of welcoming people. Some classes officially give this task to someone who naturally welcomes others.

Everyone Knows My Name

To have someone call you by name acknowledges your value. As Christians we believe that God created each person as a special and unique being, a child of God. Names are important. Learn the name of each student in your class, and help the students learn one another's names. If the class is large, use nametags, table cards, or some other method of identifying people. Always have extra nametags on hand for when a visitor or new person attends. Remember that newcomers have a lot of names to learn, so don't expect them to remember everyone's names after just one introduction.

There Is Always a Place for Me at the Table

Just as everyone is welcomed to the Communion Table, your classroom should always be a place where everyone who enters is welcomed. Be prepared for visitors, guests, and new members. Have enough Bibles, curriculum, supplies, songbooks, and chairs for those who may come.

When someone who hasn't attended for a while returns, acknowledge that you have missed him or her, but do so without causing embarrassment.

Be prepared for students with special needs. Pay attention to accessibility issues, physical limitations, and learning styles. (See *What Every Teacher Needs to Know About People*, also in this series.)

I Feel Comfortable in This Room

The room needs to fit the people who are in the class. Chairs, tables, and other furnishings should be the appropriate size for the class members.

Take into consideration the specific needs of class members, such as large-print curriculum for older adults or other people with impaired sight, an accessible room for people with physical limitations, and so forth. If some class members are experiencing declining hearing, make sure they are seated so that they can see everyone's mouths as they speak. Look for ways to minimize background noise.

Ensure that temperature, airflow, and lighting are conducive to learning.

This Is a Safe Place

Be aware of safety issues related to the classroom facilities and the class. If you teach children, make sure that nearby entrances and exits are secure to assure that children do not leave unattended and cannot be taken by unapproved adults. If you teach older adults, make certain that chairs are sturdy and not too low. Check the locations of first-aid kits and the nearest telephone in case of an emergency.

God Is Here

Both in word and in action, you and the members of the class exemplify God's presence. The presence of God is acknowledged in planned and spontaneous ways. Plan the content of the class to be consistent with the values of the class. Plan for a mix of fellowship, learning, and worship designed to help class members grow as disciples of Jesus Christ.

For Personal Reflection

Imagine that you are visiting your class for the first time. What would you experience as you entered the room? Who would greet you? What would make you feel like an outsider? What would make you feel welcomed? Write your reflections in the space below.

Physical Space

Go to your church and pretend that you are a new person in a new church. Look with new eyes as you park in the parking lot and walk to the door, down the hallways, and into your classroom. What did you observe? Was your walk interesting? Were there signs to guide your way? Did you feel welcomed and wanted? Stand in the door of your classroom. What do you see? What draws your attention? Look carefully.

If you teach young children, get down on your knees or lie down on the floor. (If the floor is too dirty for you, it is also too dirty for them.) What do the children see at that height? Listen. What do you hear? Shut your eyes and take a deep breath. What do you smell? Pay attention to your skin. Is the temperature too hot, too cold, or too humid?

If you teach older children, sit in the doorway in a chair that puts you at their height. Look around the room. Are the tables and chairs the correct height? Does the room invite the children to learn about Jesus, the Bible, and what it means to be a Christian, yet not overstimulate the senses? Is the temperature appropriate? Is there a space for the large group to gather as well as for individual and small-group activities? Is the room clean yet energizing?

If you teach youth, think about their needs. Are the chairs in your room appropriate for their growing bodies? Are there negative distractions in the room? Are there positive distractions in the room that help them focus on God, their faith, and relationships with others? Is there an area clean enough for food and drink distribution (an essential for youth)? Are there areas for conversation, for play, and for creativity? Does this room shout, "Youth belong here"?

If you teach adults, look around the space while thinking about the adults you teach. What are their needs? Is the lighting good for reading? Are the chairs comfortable without being too low? Are tables and chairs free from splinters that snag good clothing? Is the temperature of the room appropriate? Does the room invite learning? Is this a room where Christians can discuss, share, learn, and grow together?

Write down what you observe. In the course of your regular activities, it will be easy to forget your observations.

Analyze for Learning

Look around the room with your teaching team members and analyze what needs to happen to the facilities to make the room a place for learning for your class members. Identify any barriers to learning that exist in the room. Is there too much noise coming from the hallway, the room next door, or a nearby heating/air-conditioning unit? Is there something left in the room from a weekday activity that is distracting to the class? Is the temperature chronically too hot or too cold?

Consider the Class Members

Sit down at the edge of the room. Think about your students. Who are they? What are their physical needs? Does this room meet those physical needs? Are the tables and chairs the right size for your students? Older adults might need straight-back chairs with padded seats that are not too low. Six-year-olds would find adult-sized chairs uncomfortable. Is there space for three-year-olds to learn through play? Is there room for teenagers to stretch their growing bodies?

Planning for Changes

If you need to make changes to the physical space in your classroom in order to make optimal learning possible for your students, develop a plan and include the appropriate people in planning for the changes.

Talk with the Christian education director, the Sunday school superintendent, the age-level coordinator, or other people responsible for your congregation's Sunday school ministry. Explain the needs of your class and what changes you would like to make in the room. Solicit their help and advice. If the changes are cosmetic or minor, complete the changes as recommended by the Sunday school leader. If the changes are more major, ask the Sunday school leader to help you contact the Board of Trustees and make arrangements with them.

If you teach older children, teenagers, or adults, consider how they can be included in planning and fixing up their room. If the changes involve such things as painting the room and rearranging cabinetry and other furnishings, perhaps class members or parents of class members would come to a class work day to help complete the necessary tasks.

If other groups share the space during the week, including them in planning any changes may prevent long-term problems in sharing the space.

Keep the whole room in mind as you plan each class time. How can the space best be used? What limitations does the room bring? Is there anything else that might be needed in the room, or anything that should be removed? Would the class best be held in a different setting? If the response to either of the last two questions is yes, who else might need to be involved in any changes?

Stewardship of Supplies

Once your physical space is established, one of the first things to do in setting up a classroom is clean the space if it has not already been cleaned from the last class. Find out where unneeded supplies and curriculum are stored for others to share. Outdated student leaflets can be saved for children to use for cutting pictures later in the year. Adult student curriculum can be given to other classes or reused by home Bible-study groups.

Check the supply of newsprint and determine if refills are available. Sharpen pencils. Refill glue bottles. Throw away and replace dried-out markers, modeling dough, paint containers, and so forth. Gather appropriate containers for storing classroom supplies. Small, clear plastic containers with lids work great. Shoeboxes are also a good size. (Cover shoeboxes with contact paper or wrapping paper.)

Clear off shelves and clean out drawers. Clean shelf and drawer surfaces and replace supplies in an order that makes sense to you. Regularly straighten shelves and keep supplies stocked. Regularly return supplies to the common supply area as appropriate for your church so that others have access to them.

Walls and Bulletin Boards

Look at the walls in your classroom. Is there a bulletin board for you to use? Think about how you might use it as a learning tool for your classroom. In the nursery, it might be a place for parents to learn about their children. In young children's classrooms, it might be a place for pictures of Jesus, of animals, of colors, of the children themselves. In elementary children's classrooms, it might be a place to post the children's creations, photos of the children, pictures related to the curriculum, or crossword puzzles and other activities that help the children learn more about the curriculum subjects. In youth and adult classrooms, it might be a place to announce upcoming events and post photos from recent events. For more ideas, see "Bulletin Board Hints," page 19.

Bulletin Board Hints

- Change the bulletin board often if you want people to see it.
- Cover board with construction paper, table paper, newsprint, fabric, or wrapping paper.
- When using prints (fabric or wrapping paper), choose a small pattern.
- Use borders for extra appeal. Borders can be ready-made, construction paper cut into strips, paper chains, ribbon, or anything else you can imagine.
- Do not use crepe paper. It stretches and buckles.
- Display students' work and photos of the students as often as possible.
- Use curriculum pictures as appropriate, but change them often.
- Back some items on the bulletin board with colored paper to form a frame.
- Use color schemes, but change them often.
- Use bulletin boards to tell new people and classroom visitors about your class.
- Share bulletin boards with others who use the room. Use one bulletin board per group, or divide one board into sections. Renegotiate bulletin board usage each fall.

For Personal Reflection

List several things that would enhance your classroom's physical space. Make a note next to each item as to whether it is something you could do yourself or something you would need the assistance of others to do. Who could provide assistance? Choose at least one item on the list and plan how you will implement it. Write your reflections in the space below.

Spiritual Space

You and your students should feel God's presence in your classroom space. God is present when you arrive, while class is in session, and when you leave. As the teacher, it is your responsibility to assure that God is not pushed aside but is central to all that happens.

Prayer in the Classroom

Prayer is a form of communication with God. Make prayer a primary element of the curriculum plan. Be creative with prayer. Talk about prayer. Teach ways to pray. Invite class members to share prayer needs and to lead the class in prayer. Practice prayer as a regular part of class time. When you begin to teach, find out the prayer habits of the class. Encourage good habits already in place. As appropriate, teach new ways of prayer and new times for prayer. Be open to spontaneous prayer within the content of the curriculum or as conversation occurs. Pray not just at the beginning and end of class but at other times during the class. Remember that all prayer does not need to be lengthy, flowery, or even expressed verbally. Prayer can be a physical movement. Prayer can be a song. Prayer can be a poem. Prayer can be a breath or a thought. Prayer can be silence in order to hear God speak to the heart. Most important is to communicate with God as a class and as individuals within the classroom environment.

Worship Centers

Set up a worship center to create a visual reminder of God's presence. Use a table or a small stand. A worship center can be as simple as a candle or can include a cross, a Bible, an offering plate, and flowers or something else from nature.

If there is no space for a table, create a space on the wall. Use a picture that is meaningful to the class. Hang a cross. Use cloth to cover a bulletin board. Use words, pictures from past or current curriculum that are appropriate for your class, a cross, or other symbols of faith to create a focal point.

Whatever is used, change it often. Add fresh visual clues as reminders of God's presence. Change the colors to match the colors of the Christian seasons (see chart on page 23). Use symbols that relate to current curriculum or that remind the class of shared experiences with God.

Seasons of the Church Year

Season	Dates	Color	Symbols
Advent	Four Sundays before Christmas	Purple or blue	Advent wreath, Chrismon tree, Jesse tree
Christmas	December 25 to January 6	White	Nativity scene, star, angels
Season After the Epiphany	January 7 to Ash Wednesday	Green	Baptismal font, water jars, candles
Lent	Ash Wednesday to Easter	Purple	crown of thorns, nails
Easter	Easter Sunday to Pentecost	White; red for Pentecost Sunday	empty cross, butterfly
Season After Pentecost	Pentecost to Advent	Green	cross, candles, Bible

Classroom Rituals

Classroom rituals are an important part of any classroom. Whatever the class members' ages, from the youngest of children to the oldest of adults, ritual is important in reminding them of the presence of God. A ritual is something that almost always occurs and that can be relied upon to happen. It might be reciting the Lord's Prayer at the beginning of class. It might be holding hands and reciting a familiar blessing at the end of class. It might be the order in which everything happens from the beginning of class time to the end. It might be the words you use to greet students as they arrive. Rituals should reflect what is important to the class.

New rituals bring freshness. Old rituals provide comfort. Do not let rituals become stagnant. Sometimes it is good to replace a ritual with a new one. Good times for this to happen include the beginning of new curriculum or a new Christian season.

Remember the importance of rituals, but do not let rituals become a burden to the classroom environment. If you are already teaching a class, think about the rituals that have evolved. When starting to teach a class for the first time, inquire about the rituals that already exist in the class. When starting a new class in which the members have not been together, give some deliberate thought to the role of rituals. Introduce new experiences that might become rituals. Let the class help you evaluate them until the class has begun to form some rituals of their own.

For Personal Reflection

Do you have a worship center in your classroom? How long has it been since you updated it? What are your class rituals? How do these rituals help class members grow in faith? Are there some rituals that need to be changed? Write your reflections in the space below.

Social Space

Each class needs to feel as though the classroom space is their space. Knowing the class and the needs of the particular age level helps you assure that the space is appropriate for your class.

Record History

Take photographs of the class often and post them in a place where the students can check for new photos. Take a photo of any new class members to include in the photo display. From time to time, include photos taken of class members when they were younger.

Periodically, take a class photo of those present on a particular Sunday. Write their names (and ages, if appropriate) and the date of the photo on the back. Frame the photo with fadeless construction paper. At the end of your teaching time, put class photos in the church archive.

For a new class (particularly a class for very young children, the first year of youth Sunday school, or a new adult class), begin a scrapbook including class photos and other mementos. Send the scrapbook with the class when a move occurs.

Display Significant Items

For all ages, provide space on the walls or on furnishings for class symbols that have meaning for this particular class. Display class creations that are relevant to the curriculum unit currently being studied. Or invite class members to share their artistic creations with the class for a special "traveling exhibit." Do you have no place to display creative items? Build a kiosk using graduated sizes of boxes stacked on top of one another from largest up to smallest. Post your creative items on the sides of the kiosk.

Time to Talk

For adults, set up a place in the room for a coffeepot, cups, sweet rolls, napkins, and nametags for the class to access as they enter the room. You may need a gathering space for before-class and after-class conversations.

Teenagers need a place to "hang out" as they arrive. This should be a place where they can be comfortable eating doughnuts and drinking juice or soft drinks, a place where they can visit with their friends. The space should be visible and safe.

Provide children times when they are doing an activity or having a snack to talk with one another about school, pets, family activities, and so forth. Assure positive habits of conversation with friends by staying involved with the children but not dominating the conversation. Help parents know of classroom friendships. Occasionally plan a class experience away from the classroom, and include other adults for safety.

For Personal Reflection

Is there a time in your class when members have an opportunity to talk about their joys and concerns? What activities has your class done outside the regular class time? How have these activities helped your class know one another better? What could be done in your class to help create Christian community? Write your reflections in the space below.

Sharing Space

It is a common experience in the church to share classroom space with others. A preschool Sunday school classroom may be used by the weekday early childhood program of the church. The youth classroom may become a fellowship room on Sunday evenings. The young-adult classroom may be used for midweek Bible study. The parenting class may meet in the room used for receptions.

Sharing space is not always an easy experience and may create a variety of challenges. The alternative, however, is to be poor stewards of the space God has given us by letting classrooms sit empty except on Sunday mornings. As followers of Christ, we choose to share all our God-given gifts. For many Sunday school teachers, that means sharing our space with other groups throughout the week. Here are some suggestions and hints to make this sharing easier.

Allocate Storage Space

Everyone needs storage space. Evaluate space needed and space available. Advocate for additional storage if appropriate. Apportion storage space as fairly as possible. Label areas that are for common storage of supplies that will be shared. Label areas that are for storage by a specific group. Respect each other's storage, and do not borrow without permission.

Maintain a Positive Attitude

Sharing space with other people is a blessing. Pray for the people who use the room when you are not there. Ask God's blessing to be with them in the other ministries that fill the room with God's love. When irritation tries to take over your heart, pray that you will find a blessing in the room. Then strive to leave the room better than you found it as a gift to those who follow you.

Carry In

Use a portable box to store and transport your curriculum and other supplies needed each Sunday. The box can be moved from place to place, such as home, so that supplies do not have to be left in the classroom. Select a sturdy box or plastic container with handles.

Cover Up

Sometimes groups must leave large items in the room, and those items become a distraction for your class. Maybe the quilters need to leave their current project out. Or the youth group has equipment too large to put in a closet. Or the choir leaves the handbells in the corner of your room. Try covering up the distractions with an old sheet during your class time. Ask a local hotel for old sheets they are no longer using.

When my first grade Sunday school class met in a four-year-old preschool class, the tool center and kitchen center were large distractions. When we arrived on Sunday mornings, we would cover the centers with old sheets. Even though the centers were large white blobs, they became invisible to the children.

Leave Gifts

Occasionally leave a note of appreciation, a sealed bag with a cookie or piece of chocolate, a small craft item, a written prayer, or some other small gift for those who use the room after you. Mark it clearly with the name of the person it is for and leave it in an appropriate, visible place. Do not leave anything expensive.

Meet Your Neighbor

Set a time to meet with the leaders of the other groups who use the room. Get to know them. Decide together about room arrangement and rearrangements.

Exchange phone numbers. Discuss specific needs for each group. Think creatively when planning how to meet the needs of each group. Be respectful of one another. If you are going to be gone, call the person who uses the room after you and alert him or her that a substitute will be using the room.

Share Equipment

Moving things in and out for each meeting time is not easy for anyone. Make arrangements to share and to help each other, for example: "I'll leave my CD player out for others to use. You can leave nature projects for my group to appreciate. We will each contribute markers to be available for all to share."

Share Walls

It is difficult to remove everything hung on the walls after each usage. Plan with your neighbors about wall space usage. Remember the other groups when leaving drawings, letters, and pictures on the wall. Change them often. Leave them as appropriate.

Moving Into Space Each Week

If you have to totally move in and out of your space each week, plan carefully. Select lightweight containers with lids and handles to hold your supplies and curriculum. Two medium-sized containers might be better than one large container, since a large container might become too heavy and cumbersome to carry. Carry one container in to class each week. Keep the second container at home for storage of supplies. Each week, transfer supplies needed for the current week into the container that you carry in. Select smaller containers to hold supplies like crayons and scissors inside the larger boxes. Use file folders to hold curriculum. Keep containers cleaned out and organized for easy usage. When a substitute teacher will be filling in for you, make plans to transfer the containers.

For Personal Reflection

List the other groups that use your classroom space. Who are the leaders or teachers of those groups? What could you do to make sharing space a better experience for them? What could they do to make sharing space a better experience for you? How could you initiate a conversation with the other groups that you share space with? Write your reflections in the space below.

Basic Classroom Supplies

General Supply Area for All to Use

- Construction paper
- Shoeboxes
- Chalk
- Ribbon
- Yarn
- Watercolor paints
- Tempera paints
- Newsprint
- Paint shirts
- Paintbrushes
- Cardboard tubes
- Candles, matches
- Wrapping paper

- Baskets
- Lettering stencils, bulletin board letters and borders
- Rolls of white paper
- Large pieces of fabric for bulletin boards
- Seasonal puzzles
- Felt pieces and fabric scraps
- Empty margarine tubs and other containers
- Leftover miscellaneous craft supplies
- Filed posters and pictures from previous curriculum

In All Classrooms

- Bibles: Picture Bible for nursery and preschool rooms, extra Bibles for all other age levels
- Paper
- Pencils, pencil sharpener
- Curriculum resources
- Antibacterial wipes
- First-aid kit
- Offering basket
- Attendance record
- Tape
- Thumbtacks, straight pins, or pushpins
- Washable felt-tip markers
- Crayons
- Stapler and staples

Additional Items in Young Children's Classrooms

- Clean toys
- Extra diapers
- Tempera paints
- Glue

Additional Items in Elementary Children's Classrooms

- Hymnals
- Bible atlas
- Glue

Additional Items in Youth and Adult Classrooms

- Hymnals
- Bible atlas
- Newsprint
- Bible dictionary
- Concordance

Picture Files

Your church makes an investment in curriculum purchased for use each quarter. Particularly with children's curriculum, there is a packet of pictures, games, charts, and maps to use with the curriculum. If the pictures are kept and filed appropriately, they can be used repeatedly as teaching tools and as communication tools on bulletin boards and worship centers. Many of the pictures are appropriate for youth and adult classrooms, particularly those related to specific Bible stories or those that can be used for visual worship clues.

For Personal Reflection

When was the last time you inventoried the supplies in your class? Are there supplies that need to be replenished? Are there extra supplies that need to be returned to the general supply area? Are there supplies that you need that someone in the church might want to donate? Write your reflections in the space below.

Going Further

As you become more aware of how your classroom environment enhances the faith formation of your class members, you may want to experiment with new ways of arranging your classroom space and creative uses of wall space.

Think about ways that your classroom can extend beyond its walls. Can you use the hallways to create a mural that relates to the Bible stories being studied or to display student work?

Members of your class, or parents of members if you teach children, may be talented in creating visuals. Invite them to use their gifts; you do not have to do everything yourself. Some churches have a ministry group with the responsibility of creating hallway bulletin boards and visuals that relate to the season of the church year or to the subjects being studied in Sunday school.

It is important to pay attention to the physical classroom environment. However, as important as that is, paying attention to the needs of the students is imperative. Changing the bulletin board before Sunday school begins is not nearly as important as listening to the needs of the student who arrives early. Whenever it is necessary to make a decision between the classroom and the needs of a student, place the student first every time.

Helpful Resources

Websites

General Board of Discipleship of The United Methodist Church (www.gbod.org). On this site you will find articles related to discipleship and teaching. Particular sites of interest are those on Christian Education (www.gbod.org/education), Children's Ministries (www.gbod.org/children), Youth Ministries (www.gbod.org/youth), Family Ministries (www.gbod.org/family), Generational Studies (www.gbod.org/generation) and Keeping in Touch (www.gbod.org/keepingintouch.)

Discipleship Resources (www.discipleshipresources.org). In this online bookstore you can purchase additional copies of this booklet, other booklets in the series, and other books published by Discipleship Resources.

Books

The First Three Years: A Guide for Ministry With Infants, Toddlers, and Two-Year-Olds, edited by Mary Alice Gran (Discipleship Resources, revised 2001). This book includes a variety of articles on classroom environment for young children.

Keeping in Touch: Christian Formation and Teaching, by Carol F. Krau (Discipleship Resources, 1999). Looks at the role of the teacher in creating faith-forming classrooms.

Out of the Basement: A Holistic Approach to Children's Ministry, by Diane C. Olson (Discipleship Resources, 2001). Looks at the systems needed to create a healthy church environment for children.

Safe Sanctuaries: Reducing the Risk of Child Abuse in the Church, by Joy Thornburg Melton (Discipleship Resources, 1998). Helps congregations develop policies and procedures to ensure a safe church environment.

Start Here: Teaching and Learning With Adults, by Barbara Bruce (Discipleship Resources, 2000). Provides helpful information for creating a faith-forming environment in adult classrooms.

Teaching Young Children: A Guide for Teachers and Leaders, by MaryJane Pierce Norton (Discipleship

Resources, 1997 revised). For teachers who teach infants up to first grade. Includes teaching tips and classroom information.

Ordering Information

Resources published by Discipleship Resources may be ordered online at www.discipleshipresources.org; by phone at 800-685-4370; by fax at 770-442-9742; or by mail from Discipleship Resources Distribution Center, P.O. Box 1616, Alpharetta, GA 30009-1616.